FIFTY WAYS TO LEARN A LANGUAGE

SHANE DIXON

JUSTIN SHEWELL

WAYZGOOSE PRESS

CONTENTS

HOW TO USE THIS BOOK

The activities here were selected based on several criteria:

1. The activity must be, above all, academically sound. Thus, these activities all have roots, although sometimes contested, in research-based concepts.
2. The activity must be, on the whole, motivational. While not every activity will be exciting or interesting to every learner, we have carefully chosen activities that represent something that most learners will want to try. You may notice that there is a sort of "adventure" quality to these activities, and in fact, we refer to them as "mini language adventures."
3. Each and every activity should be 'level-agnostic,' meaning that whether you are a beginner or advanced learner of the language, these activities can provide positive results.

So pick a language, pick an activity, and start learning immediately.

As you read the following activities, keep in mind the following suggestions:

- **Review all 50 tips again and again**. These ideas can be read in any order, and an idea that might sound daunting or uninteresting in one moment might feel possible and even exciting later on. Thus, getting basic familiarity with these ideas is a good way to start. Make your favorite activities a regular part of your language-learning diet.
- **Use the back page**. The back page provides a summary of all 50 tips to quickly remind you of all the possible activities.
- **Work with others.** One way to make this book really interesting is to invite or challenge others on social media (Facebook, Instagram, or Twitter, for example) to complete an activity with you. Ask them to not only join you but also post their results. It is amazing what a little collaboration – or friendly competition – can do. And who knows? Your enthusiasm might encourage someone else to take up a foreign language as well!
- **Be kind to yourself.** You might have had previous discouraging experiences with trying to learn a foreign language. But don't let your past define you. You are not 'stupid' or 'bad at languages.' You simply weren't ready before; and now you are. If one method doesn't work for

you, it doesn't mean you can't learn – it means you need a different method. That's why we give you a wide variety of techniques and approaches in this book. Celebrate your successes, and forgive your mistakes. Having a positive mindset will make learning easier, faster – and a lot more enjoyable!

INTRODUCTION

tonga soa
välkommen 환영 velkommen നുഗന്ദു

bienvenida dobrodošli
خوش آمد gaidīts bienvenu
स्वागत herzlich willkommen
fáilte roimh benvenuto bun venit
добро пожаловать
selamat datang тавтай морилно уу ברוכים karşılama
maraba welcome 欢迎
fogadtatás
ยินดีต้อนรับ добродошао welkom vitejte
bemvindo
bienvenue വരവേൽപ്പ് καλωσόρισμα
maligayang pagdating वेलकम श्रागॸ kuwakaribisha vitajte
powitanie hoan nghênh

This book is for learners of any language. The book is intended to not only teach strategies but to give motivation and structure to someone who simply doesn't know where to start. In other words, this book is a sort of primer, meaning a preparatory series of strategies, for language learning.

A *language learner strategy* is an activity or process that is used to help you to more effectively conquer a language. Many language experts and social scientists classify these strategies into categories such as, but not limited to:

- social (make a friend who speaks the language)
- emotional (talk to yourself in the mirror and tell yourself you can do it)
- cognitive (rehearse a conversation in your head before you speak)
- metacognitive (reflect on what you said after a presentation).

This short book will give you a variety of activities that spans these different types of language learner strategies.

Learning another language can be such an over-whelming goal that many people quit before they begin. Thus, language learner strategies, at least like the ones offered here, help a learner overcome fears by giving them small "bite-sized" opportunities to engage in a foreign language. Besides their economical size, good language learner strategies also help a learner recognize ways in which a language can be more appropriately and efficiently mastered.

As you go through these 50 tips, keep in mind the following pieces of advice:

- **Language learning is eating an elephant.** *How do you eat an elephant?* asks the old joke. *One bite* *at a time*. Because language learning is so large, it is best to do small, consistent activities daily in order to improve. It is consistent effort over time that creates success.

- **Language learning is basketball.** Recognize that language is not learned by putting your head in a book, but by getting your head in the game. What we mean is, language is best put to use. You forget what you learn, but you acquire what you practice.

- **Language learning is cake.** Language learning can be a particularly painful process when you are not in charge of the material. Make sure you are learning material that is interesting to you. This may be very different from what is interesting to others, but that is okay. Remember that language learning can be a delicious experience, and it doesn't *have* to feel like school.

- **Language learning is a camera.** Finally, in *Strategies for Success*, H. Douglas Brown rightly informs us to think of language learning as a camera with two lenses: a zoom lens for looking at language from a detailed, narrow perspective, and a wide-angle lens for looking at the broader picture. Some learners focus on grammar points or single vocabulary words and never lose themselves in the joy of conversation. They are so focused on the trees that they cannot enjoy the forest, so to speak. Others enjoy conversation so much that they never correct specific grammar points or vocabulary words.

They are thinking only about the forest and can't see the individual beauty of each tree. In other words, good language learners often take a balanced approach, sometimes focusing on the rhythm of language without stressing out over every word or phrase, and sometimes paying attention to the small details that they haven't yet acquired. This book presents activities that invite both a zoom lens and wide-angle lens approach.

❧ I ❧

ADVENTURE STARTERS

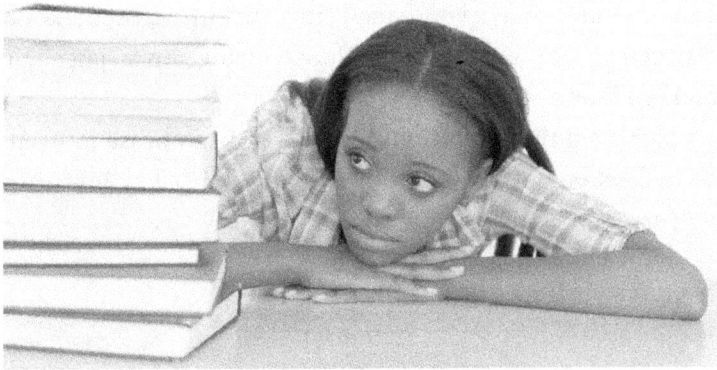

Have you ever set a goal and felt really excited to begin working on achieving it, only to realize several weeks later that you are no closer than you were before? For many people, learning a language is something they've always wanted to do. They think about, they talk about it, but there is very little action because they don't know where to begin.

The mini language adventures in this section will help you begin your language learning journey right now. These are things you can do immediately, and every day, to help you start learning a new language.

~

1. INVEST IN YOUR LANGUAGE.

What does it mean to *invest* in language? Well, buying a ticket to France would certainly increase your daily motivation to study French, but not everyone can just buy a ticket. But don't fret—a number of motivational studies demonstrate that even small investments can make a difference. For example, put loose change in a glass jar marked "Paris."

Not even that ambitious? Buy a book, a phrase journal, or make some other small investment that tells your brain you are committed to your own success.

2. MEMORIZE SOMETHING COOL.

Whether it be a lengthy poem, a favorite passage in a book, or the lyrics to a song, memorizing something you love can give you insights into the language that you wouldn't get otherwise. A careful focus on how certain words are put together can really help to establish patterns of language early on.

Make this a social activity by reciting (or singing!) to a friend. One learner actually sang a song they memorized in their target language on TV while traveling in a country where that language was spoken. Who knows where memorizing something cool will take you!

3. CREATE A TO-DO LIST.

Creating a to-do list will force you to use everyday words for everyday items that you *actually* use. So a to-do list, like a shopping list or a chores list, will get you involved with the words you need and use right now. Finding and using authentic language is one of the keys to future success.

4. APP IT UP IN YOUR DOWNTIME.

While a language app is not a total solution for language learning, it can be particularly useful during those moments when you aren't doing anything. On a bus headed home? Have 10 minutes to kill at a doctor's appointment? The times in between are often great moments to take advantage of learning a language.

Download at least one or two and see which one grabs you. Duolingo (http://www.duolingo.com) and FluentU (https://www.fluentu.com) are two of the most popular.

5. LEARN THROUGH MUSIC.

Music is often someone's first introduction into another language or culture. Often you can find not only a song you like but the lyrics that accompany that song online. Spend time studying by listening to the song and then trying to understand the words. It can be exciting to discuss and argue over the meaning of your favorite lyrics with your language partners.

6. IMPRESS WITH RANDOM PHRASES.

When one learner was in Korea, he learned a phrase that basically means *as much as a rat's tail* (meaning *not very much*). When people would ask how much Korean he knew, he would say, in all honesty, "as much as a rat's tail." It made Koreans laugh, broke the ice, and even impressed them with his knowledge of such a random phrase. This helped motivate him to continue learning new phrases and finding opportunities to use them in general conversation.

❦ 2 ❦

ADVENTURES IN FOOD

We love food. Food is something that brings people together and makes us feel closer to our family and friends. Food is enjoying new smells and tastes, and having new and unique experiences. Food is culture and transcends cultures. And yes, food is a great facilitator for language learning.

The mini language adventures that follow will help you use food as a gateway to new experiences in a new language.

～

7. MAKE A DINNER.

One way to motivate yourself to speak your target language is to make food from the target culture. Food is a great way to overcome language barriers. Invite your friends over. People love to talk about food.

Preparing cuisine from a culturally specific place also gives you an immediate conversation topic. You can learn the names of the dishes you've prepared, or the ingredients in your target language and teach them to your friends.

8. USE A RECIPE IN YOUR TARGET LANGUAGE.

We have already discussed the social benefits of how great it is to make a food from another culture and invite people over to discuss it, but there is also a great cognitive benefit to following a recipe in a target language.

Recipes follow typical patterns, such as serving sizes and basic commands. You'll learn a lot of language just by following a few recipes, and that language is controlled in a way that makes it easier to learn.

9. GO SOMEPLACE THAT LOVES YOUR LANGUAGE WITH SOMEONE WHO LOVES YOUR LANGUAGE.

Most often, this means a good restaurant. While it is always fun to talk to someone who knows the language you're learning, going with them to a place that embodies that language and culture can be a way of easily inviting topics, sharing interests, and picking up useful bits of real language.

The person you go with doesn't even have to speak your target language that well. They just need to be willing to speak in the target language with you. At the very least, you can share a good meal!

❧ 3 ❧
LANGUAGE WATCHING
ADVENTURES

These days, it is all about video. We see video everywhere we turn – on the Internet, in our social media feeds, on our phones, and of course, on television. Have you ever thought of using all those resources to learn a language? Watching videos in a foreign language, taking a language course through video, or watching videos about your target language's culture are great ways to help you progress and motivate yourself in your language learning journey.

The following mini language adventures help you make use of those vast video resources to learn a language.

~

10. LISTEN TO COMMERCIALS IN A DIFFERENT LANGUAGE.

One of the great things about listening to commercials, especially commercials for products that you are familiar with (say, Coca Cola, for example) is that they often do a lot of work to help you understand them, regardless of language. That makes listening and watching commercials an excellent opportunity to pick up pieces of language.

Commercials are a fun way to see (and pick up) the rhythm of informal language. You can find a host of foreign language commercials on YouTube.

11. GO ON A YOUTUBE BINGE.

YouTube has become an excellent playground for language learning, and there are a number of YouTube stars that post videos in bite-sized chunks. Comments below the videos are sometimes good resources as well.

Don't forget, in a video, you can pause or repeat, giving you multiple chances to understand things a little bit more easily.

EasyLanguages (https://www.youtube.com/user/magauchsein) is a great place to begin.

12. MAKE IT FOREIGN FILM NIGHT.

Many online streaming services such as Netflix (http://www.netflix.com), Hulu (http://www.hulu.com), and Amazon Prime (http://www.primevideo.com) have movies that are available in dozens of other languages, often with English and/or other language subtitles to assist you.

Watching a movie — or even better, a series — can be a way of learning about a culture, picking up language as you go along, and immersing yourself in the sounds of another language.

Feeling like you aren't picking anything up? Taking a notebook along and writing down phrases you hear and want to study later can give this relaxed activity a little structure.

13. WATCH A TED TALK IN YOUR TARGET LANGUAGE. WRITE DOWN WORDS YOU WANT TO LEARN.

Did you know that some of the most famous TED talks (http://www.ted.com/) are available in dozens of languages through closed captioning? TED talks are often inspiring and can help motivate you and make you think.

In addition, TED talks often provide full transcripts in multiple languages, which help you compare your language to the target.

Don't know where to start? Ask your social media group to share *their* favorite TED talk.

14. FIND A SHOW YOU ALREADY KNOW AND REDISCOVER IT IN YOUR TARGET LANGUAGE.

Do you love the series *Friends*? *House of Cards*? *Game of Thrones*? *Seinfeld*? *Full House*? These shows and more are available in other languages. If you have a favorite show, look for it in your target language.

Teachers and researchers recognize that when learners understand the context of a conversation, it becomes much easier to acquire the vocabulary and grammar. How does Joey say "How *you* doin'?" in German, anyway?

15. WATCH A MOVIE TRAILER. TRY TO DO 'THAT' VOICE.

There are movie trailers that are translated into dozens of languages. In movie trailers, you will usually hear modern, current language. Since movie trailers often have a dramatic element to them, you can pick up phrases that you wouldn't otherwise encounter.

In a world...

4

AT HOME ADVENTURES

They say that "home is where the heart is," and this is true for language learning as well. If your heart is truly in your language learning experience, it will manifest itself in your home as well. Part of learning any language is creating an environment where you are encouraged and given opportunities to use it for meaningful communication. These mini language adventures will help you turn your home into a place where your language learning flourishes.

∾

16. MAKE A LANGUAGE ZONE.

Making a language zone in your house can be quite motivating. Having a language chair or even a language room is one way to not only encourage not only yourself but get others involved. Make your language zone official by posting a sign that states, "Language zone: Only Japanese spoken here!"

Make sure you speak the target language as much as you can in your language zone, and maybe even set up system of rewards for when other people speak your target language there.

17. STICKY NOTE YOUR HOME.

Use sticky notes (like Post-it® notes) to label objects throughout your home. Sticky notes can transform the most mundane home into a language-learning ecosystem. The visual and geographic aspect of sticky notes make it much easier to remember...and you can have other house members to collaborate with you!

Once you commit a word to memory, simply remove the note. To make the task manageable, you could choose a certain number of words per room (say, ten or twelve); after you remove one that you've learned, add another new one.

18. TALK TO FIDO.

We aren't actually suggesting you have a conversation with an animal – what we're referring to here is called a *think aloud*. Have you ever spoken to yourself in preparation for an important presentation or speech? Then you know what a think aloud is. A number of polyglots swear by this technique.

Put simply, in a think aloud, you find a location where you are comfortable speaking to yourself as if you were having a conversation. Many language learners use think alouds while driving to work, waiting for a bus, or even with a family pet.

Is there a chance that you might look crazy? Sure. That's why we recommend Fido... to hide the fact that you are, well, literally talking to yourself. Good dog, Fido.

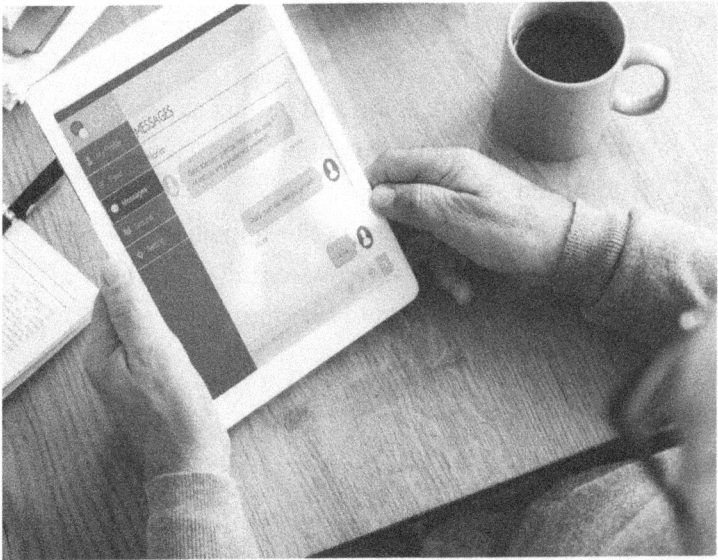

5

ADVENTURES IN SOCIAL MEDIA

For many people, social media is a major part of any day, and it may be where they interact most with friends and family. Incorporating your social media activities into your language learning journey provides many readily accessible opportunities for you to both produce and understand information in your target language.

The following adventures will help you take advantage of your social media resources to spur your language learning along.

~

19. POST A VIDEO ON YOUR SOCIAL MEDIA PAGE.

With the advent of the Internet, language learning has never been easier. Connecting yourself to others by posting a video can be a great way to accomplish two goals:

1. It forces you to prepare and perfect a certain amount of language, which is definitely an important skill to acquire.
2. It allow others who speak the language (or who are learning it just like you) to find you. Think of it as a homing beacon to like-minded adventurers.

20. WRITE A STATUS UPDATE.

It is fun to write mysteriously. Writing in a foreign language gives other people a chance to figure out what you are trying to say. It can involve others in a non-intrusive way. Even a simple post like, "I'm really tired today" can inspire people to respond to you in a way they wouldn't ordinarily.

You can also write bilingual posts if you prefer. Post first in English, and then in your target language (use a dictionary for help if necessary). That way, none of your friends will be left out, and you'll be learning and practicing the language that is most meaningful and useful to you.

21. FOLLOW AN INTERNATIONAL CELEBRITY.

Twitter (http://www.twitter.com)
Instagram (http://www.instagram.com)
YouTube (http://www.youtube.com)
Facebook (http://www.facebook.com) and other forms of social media can give you a chance to keep up with a famous celebrity.

By doing so, you will receive language that is often, well, 280 characters or less. These bite-sized chunks, given to you by someone you want to know better, may be the perfect way for you to pick up key words and ideas.

22. CONSIDER REDDIT.

Reddit (http://www.reddit.com) is a website that provides instant and immediate conversation about any topic all the time. It is a discussion that basically never ends. And that, of course, can be a powerful way to learn a language.

You can ask any question you want:

- *Can someone help me learn Thai verb conjugations?*
- *Does anyone know of a good book for intermediate German?*
- *What's a good children's book to read in Korean?*

In addition, you can follow groups that are interested in the same language you are. As just one example, if you're learning French, you might want to subscribe to threads like these:

http://reddit.com/r/learnfrench
http://reddit.com/r/French
http://reddit.com/r/france

23. JOIN A LANGUAGE CLUB ON SOCIAL MEDIA.

Going to social media and joining groups is often a simple way to make a friend. While there are language clubs that can help you find language-minded partners, you can also find success by joining groups about music, food, or popular culture. Learning Spanish and love Antonio Banderas? Join his fan club and chat about his upcoming movie.

24. WASTE TIME.

Many of us have those moments in time when we are

simply waiting – waiting at a doctor's office, waiting for your kids to come home, waiting for the mail to come.

At times like these, it is nice to have something fun to do in your target language. Make it frivolous; even silly. Watch bloopers of people falling, stupid cat videos, and whatever else you have wasted your life on before.

But whatever you might search for on the phone or computer, *this* time, commit to doing it in a different language. With language learning as your primary goal, you can waste your time with just a little less guilt.

6

ADVENTURES WITH FRIENDS

Doing something with friends can be more enjoyable than doing it alone, and this is true with language learning as well. Involving your friends in your language adventures gives you people to communicate with and have fun with, and it makes you accountable for your progress because your friends will be interested in what you've learned and how you're progressing.

These next adventures will help you find ways to learn language with friends both old and new.

∼

25. WRITE 7 NOTES TO 7 FRIENDS IN 7 DAYS...IN THE TARGET LANGUAGE.

This is a great strategy to challenge someone to do with you. It's also fun to select the seven lucky people with whom you might want to write in the target language.

One learner mentioned how she sent letters in Spanish to all of her high school friends, none of whom spoke any Spanish (except that they had all been in her Spanish class). A number of her friends wrote her back...in Spanish. Many of them loved her creativity and wanted to learn what and why she had written to them in these personal, mysterious notes.

26. FIND AN INTERNET LESSON AND TAKE IT WITH A FRIEND.

Language lessons are found all over the Internet, and some of the best ones provide videos, clear explanations of grammar, vocabulary, and pronunciation, as well as practice material for you to test out your skills.

If you find a lesson or two you like, you may feel ambitious enough to take an entire course. Ready to do so? Then remember that joining a course with a friend often improves the experience by giving you a much needed discussion partner and the motivation to finish.

Was the lesson terrible? Then think about why it didn't work and take mental notes as to what it is that would truly help you. When there is something you cannot find, there is still a chance it will bring wisdom to your mind.

27. SKYPE A FRIEND.

Take a pen pal friendship to the next level by meeting them over Skype (http://www.skype.com). Skype (or other face-to-face chat services) gives you a chance to practice your speaking with people you already know. It's usually best to have a conversation topic already picked out and a series of questions to keep the conversation going, like these topics here: Conversation Questions for the ESL/EFL classroom (http://iteslj.org/questions/). Make sure you only speak the target language, at least as much as you can.

What if you don't know anyone you can Skype with? You could try using The Mixxer (https://www.language-exchanges.org) to find language partners over Skype. This service will help connect you with someone looking to learn your native language while you try to learn theirs.

7

READ YOUR OWN ADVENTURE

A lot of people think that they can't read in their target language until they've learned enough to be conversationally fluent. While being fluent might be required to read in a foreign language as well as you do in your native language, reading in your target language even at the beginning of your language learning adventure provides some excellent benefits.

Reading will help you learn new vocabulary and grammar, while at the same time allowing you to take it at your own pace. You can translate it, dissect it, put it back together at your own speed, and have fun while doing it.

These next adventures focus on ways to incorporate reading into your language learning journey.

∾

28. READ A WIKIPEDIA ARTICLE IN YOUR LANGUAGE AND THE TARGET LANGUAGE.

Wikipedia (http://www.wikipedia.org) is a know-it-all. Take advantage of this fact by reading information you would like to know, and then reading that same information in a different language. Wikipedia often gives identical or close to identical information on similar topics. Want to learn about Italy in Italian? Go right ahead!

29. FIND A NEWSPAPER/NEWSFEED IN A FOREIGN LANGUAGE AND SUBSCRIBE TO IT.

Newspapers and newsfeeds give you up-to-date information on themes you may be naturally interested in. Besides topics you have familiarity with already, you will find that foreign language newspapers and newsfeeds tell you about situations you had never considered. Such news sources are useful to broaden your horizons and increase your desire to visit the world.

For some of you, it may be too hard to understand much of the news in a different language. If so, pay attention to just the headlines or advertisements. Make it a game to see what you *can* understand. You can always use an online dictionary to translate a few key words for help.

30. READ A CLASSIC.

Instead of a textbook, find a copy of a popular book that has been translated in multiple languages. It might be a favorite novel like *The Little Prince* or a Harry Potter novel. It might be a religious text (the Koran for devout Muslims, for example, or the Bible for a devout Christian). It might even be something terribly simple, like Dr. Seuss' *The Cat in the Hat* (which has been translated into more than a hundred languages, including Latin and Yiddish).

Find a copy of an interesting text in your target language and read it alongside a copy in your native language.

31. TEXTBOOK HOP.

Instead of following your textbook in order, prioritize the topics you are interested in and study by jumping around. Language isn't a static process, so you don't have to be static in your approach. You will often find that a targeted approach to grammar gives you the best results.

Don't have a textbook? Then consider picking one up online or at a bookstore. You might want to check with your fellow language learners to see what they can recommend (or lend).

※ 8 ※

WRITE YOUR OWN ADVENTURE

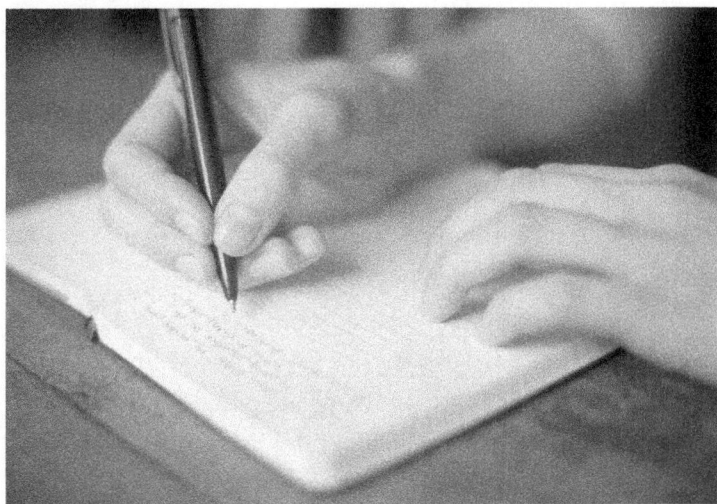

Just like with reading, many people wait until they feel they are more fluent in a language to begin learning how to write in that language, but this excludes them from the many wonderful opportunities they might have to communicate with people in their target language in written form.

It's much easier to write something in a social media post or an email than it is to record a video and send it to someone, for example. Similarly, if you need to leave someone a note, you would typically write it down instead of speaking it. You don't have to be fluent in a language in order to learn to write in that language.

These next adventures will help you begin writing in your target language.

~

32. REWRITE YOUR LAST EMAIL IN A DIFFERENT LANGUAGE.

There is something to the art of saying something you have already said in a different language. Try to translate a talk, a blog, an email, or even some text messages and try to write in the target language.

You may need to rely on a good dictionary, as well as translating apps such as Linguee (http://www.linguee.com) or Google Translate (https://translate.google.com).

These won't be entirely accurate, but will be a point of departure. You'll find that you become better at identifying words you are likely to use anyway since you are looking up vocabulary in your own voice.

33. WRITE A LOVE LETTER.

Practice your creative skills by seeing if you can write a poem or love letter to your significant other. This will test your ability to not only compose with good grammar, but also to communicate a message that shows what you love about someone else. Getting a romantic message in another language? Twice as romantic!

34. KEEP A LANGUAGE JOURNAL.

The idea here is that you are writing about everyday things in your target language. You could, for example, write about upcoming events or ones you recently attended. You might take a walk and just record what you see.

Whatever you do, make it interesting or useful — or both! Your journal is a place for you to record words and grammar structures you have learned and practice using them, as well as a place for you to practice expressing ideas in the language you are learning.

❧ 9 ❧

STRANGE(R) ADVENTURES

Chances are, if you're learning a new language, not many of your friends and family will speak that language. That means you'll need to go outside your comfort zone and make new friends. Talking and interacting with people you don't know is often scary and demotivating for people.

This next set of adventures is designed to help you comfortably talk to strangers and make new friends, while interacting in your target language.

$\sim$

35. SEARCH FOR SUCCESSFUL LANGUAGE LEARNERS.

When you look for language learners around you, look everywhere. Look at work, in your family, online, at church, and in social groups. As you do so, you will realize that many times, people you know share your same language interest.

As you look for language learners, you may also have to expand your circle of friends. Which means, well, more friends! Fellow language learners are like comrades in arms, willing to help you out. They often have access to books, movies, and other tangible resources you might use. The most tangible resource? Someone to talk to!

36. TRY THE 'GLASS CLINK' METHOD.

Benny Lewis, *National Geographic*'s Traveler of the Year, has the ability to strike up a conversation with just about anyone, and suggests this method for overcoming your fear. He says it this way: "The most important thing I think about when I approach someone new is...nothing." Along this line of thinking, he invented the "glass clink method."

What is the glass clink method? Well, Lewis was once speaking to a German woman who wished to start up a conversation in English with a group of Americans. Benny took her by the hand, directed her to a group of people, had her clink glasses with each member of the group, and then left her alone. She reports that after overcoming her initial fear, she had a marvelous time.

Don't have a dinner party to attend? How about that one person that speaks the language better than you that you don't want to talk with because you get oh, so nervous? Yes, talk with *that* person. Find out more at https://www.fluentin3months.com/shy-solution.

37. MINGLE ONLINE.

There are a number of places on the Internet that are especially designed for language learners to meet up. Places like Verbling (https://www.verbling.com), Language Partners (https://www.mylanguageexchange.com/Default.asp), Live Lingua (https://www.livelingua.com), and Italki (https://www.italki.com/home) provide opportunities for you to meet fellow language learners.

However, that's not the only place to mingle and learn online. There are also places that aren't language related, but where internationally minded people go to talk, such as InterNations (https://www.internations.org) and MeetUp (https://www.meetup.com).

38. ASK THE UNIVERSE FOR A LANGUAGE PARTNER.

Asking social media to provide you a language partner may sound a bit like making a wish and throwing a coin into a fountain. However, you might be surprised which people you know speak your target language whether fluent or just a little, and you might be even more surprised to discover there are people you don't know who are willing to help.

If no one responds? Increase your social media presence by joining language groups and finding like-minded individuals.

39. FIND AND BE THE 'NEXT LEVEL UP.'

Finding someone who exceeds your skill is an important task. Why? It gives you a resource that you can rely on, someone who has information you can glean. For example, if you are taking a 100-level Chinese class at the university, try getting tutored by someone finishing a 200 level course.

But don't forget to pay it forward as well. What does that mean? Well, just like it is important to find a mentor, it is important to be one. Being a mentor can give you excellent practice and can help solidify your learning. So remember to spend some time asking a question or two to someone who exceeds your language skill, and then help someone else by answering his or her questions.

40. FIND AN INTERNATIONAL PEN PAL.

You may already know people from around the world that speak the language you are hoping to learn. However, if you are looking for a specific language partner and can't seem to find anyone that speaks that language, there are websites specifically designed just for you. Choose your favorite search engine and type, "international pen pal." You'll find dozens of sites that might help you out.

Already have a pen pal? Send your pen pal a thank you note and write what you appreciate about your friendship.

41. PLAY GAMES WITH STRANGERS.

While your mother might have told you to be wary of strangers, the truth is that the online world allows us to take a few more chances to meet and interact with people we don't know. If you have a favorite online game, you might wish to try to find an opponent who speaks your target language. Scrabble in Spanish? Why not? You'll find that playing games is a completely different kind of language study, and one that allows you to relax and enjoy yourself.

Don't know of any games? Do a simple Google search that includes the word "game" and your target language.

42. PLAY "I SPY" WITH SOMEONE WHO KNOWS THE FOREIGN LANGUAGE.

The game "I Spy" is a common game families play while on the road. It's also an excellent language learning game that can improve your ability to identify authentic vocabulary in the world around you.

The game is played by having the foreign language speaker choose an object that is visible to everyone in the room. He or she then gives a clue about the object selected by saying, "I spy something (purple; big; small; round)." The foreign language speaker starts simple, with words that the group is probably familiar with. Dictionaries may be used when the words get more complicated.

Don't have a group to play with? Play "I Spy" by yourself by simply looking around, wherever you are, and seeing how many words you know (or don't know). You can group them by category to make the task more manageable — for example, see if you can name all the *blue* objects in the room, and then all the objects *made of wood*. Make a note of the words you don't know and make an effort to learn them.

LANGUAGE LEARNING
STRATEGIES

Technically, these are not so much mini language adventures as they are strategies to help you as you progress along your language-learning journey. These strategies are taken from research on what good language learners do as well as from the personal experience of the authors and those they know who've learned one or more foreign languages. Use these strategies to improve your study and have fun!

~

43. STUDY LANGUAGE-LEARNING STRATEGIES.

Consider improving and expanding your strategies. Rather than just studying a language, consider figuring out *how* to study a language. 'Language learning strategies' is a phrase worthy of a Google search, and if you look carefully, you'll love getting good ideas from others. Don't be afraid to ask successful language learners what strategies worked best for them. (P.S. This book itself has 51 of them, but there are many more.)

44. LEARN TO CHUNK.

It is frustrating to encounter something you don't under-stand in a language. Many learners discover that watching a movie in another language is simply impossible. It is too long, too hard, and too fast. If this is the case with some-thing you encounter, try "chunking."

Chunking means that you take a bite-sized piece of the whole (let's say, 5 minutes of the movie), and spend time reviewing it multiple times. You might want to find a beginning, middle, and end, and work on each section you have blocked off for yourself.

Many learners discover that chunking helps them discover new ways to learn a language. Chunking can be fun – just remember to slow it down, split it up, and repeat. And this doesn't just work for watching a movie. If you're going to memorize a poem or speech, this is a must-do technique.

45. COMPARE YOUR SPEECH TO NATIVE-LIKE SPEECH.

Trying to imitate a small conversation is an excellent way to focus on pronunciation. But often you don't get feedback or hints that help you improve your mistakes. This is where having a partner who is above your current level can be key, and having a native speaker friend even better.

No one around? You might want to investigate websites such as Babbel (https://www.babbel.com). Don't want to make that kind of commitment just yet? Try the constantly improving Google Translate (https://translate.google.com), which will pronounce words and phrases for you.

46. ASSIGN A TIME.

This technique is a must for people who think they don't have enough time. Establishing a pattern so that language learning happens every day is simply one of the primary keys for polyglots all over the world. Want to learn languages? Then you must be naturally insatiable but patient, and adventurous but steady.

Setting a time each day, however, may be too rigid for you, so you may want to set a time limit – say, 15 minutes a day – and then see if you can exceed that limit. Give yourself a treat if you achieve your weekly goal. Ice cream is always part of a good language learning plan.

47. CREATE FLASHCARDS.

Creating your own flashcards helps you better retain the vocabulary you study because you have to write a definition that makes sense to you, and you can include a picture that represents that word for you. These tasks help strengthen the neural pathways in your brain and improve your recall of learned vocabulary words. Make sure you have a friend quiz you on your flashcards.

Want to create flashcards online? Try Quizlet (http://www.quizlet.com).

48. STUDY IN A LANGUAGE, AND STOP STUDYING LANGUAGE.

Hardly anyone learns a language for the sake of just learning a language. Language is a gateway; a path to encounter a world of fun, culture, and exploration. Do you enjoy skiing, gardening, classic literature, hip-hop, car repair, or, well, anything at all? Come on, there *has* to be something.

The truth is, we learn a language because it allows us to interact. Use that fact to your benefit by choosing to learn *about* something in another language, rather than just the language itself. Finding real interests will inspire you to figure out difficult vocabulary, uncover the meaning of grammatically impossible structures, and get the information that you want.

Don't have any interests? Then we suggest that you get off the couch right now and become more interesting.

49. CREATE MNEMONIC DEVICES TO REMEMBER VOCABULARY.

Sometimes vocabulary can be a bit tricky to remember. For difficult words, often a mnemonic device can help. First, think of the word, then think of an English equivalent for that word and create a crazy association with it.

For example, in Spanish, the word *dormir* means "to sleep"—so you might imagine telling someone, "**Mere**ly close the **door** before you go to bed" to remember *dormir*.

Or with the word "money" (*dinero*), you might think: "I wish I had as much money as Robert *Dinero*."

This technique can also be applied to learning the written characters in languages such as Arabic and Japanese. For example, the Japanese character for /ku/, as in *cuckoo bird*, looks like a beak: < . So picturing a *cuckoo* each time you see the Japanese kanji "ku" (<) can improve your memory.

50. MAKE A PLAN!

Making a plan helps you focus on the overall goal and the steps you need to take in order to get there. Include things you want to learn, and tasks you want to be able to do in your language plan. Include a realistic timeframe and plan out what you will do at each phase of your language learning journey to continually progress toward your goal. You might even include rewards you want to give yourself when you reach certain mini-goals along the way.

Don't have any idea how to make a plan? Download a free individual language plan from http://language-warriors.com/ilp.pdf

BONUS TIP!

51. KEEP A LANGUAGE LEARNING JOURNAL

A language learning journal is a journal kept in your native language that details your successes and failures in learning a language. It's a way to share which learner strategies you enjoyed most and which ones truly helped you learn.

Above all, it's a way to reflect on and share your story. The more you think about your audience, the better you will be at spreading the gospel of language learning to others.

Language learning stories are naturally interesting, and can provide genuine insight into how language is truly acquired.

ADDITIONAL RESOURCES

SOME RESOURCES WORTHY OF A "LANGUAGE ADVENTURE":

• **BBC Languages** – An extensive resource covering some of the most popular languages and cultures.
   (http://www.bbc.co.uk/languages)

• **Mac Genius** – Genius helps you memorize things. Genius organizes your information and carefully chooses questions using an intelligent "spaced repetition" method that's based on your past performance.
   (http://www.macupdate.com/app/mac/13938/genius).

• **Anki** – Anki is a program that makes remembering things easy, which works on PC. It is a lot more efficient than traditional study methods. You can either greatly decrease your time spent studying or greatly increase the amount you learn.

(http://ankisrs.net).

• **Talking Translator/Dictionary** (Android & IOS) –
Speak a sentence and hear the translation in the language
of your choice; plus many other useful features.
   (https://play.google.com/store/apps/details?
id=com.greenleaf.android.translator.enes.a&hl=en)

~

References

Brown, H. D. (2002). *Strategies for success: a practical
guide to learning English*. White Plains, NY.: Longman.
   Lewis, B. (2014). *Fluent in 3 months*. London: Collins.

Shane Dixon, Ph.D., Senior Global Educator, Arizona State University

Dr. Dixon has 20 years of TESOL experience, and has taught in Venezuela, Mexico, Iraq, and the US. He has helped designed teacher training programs for groups from China, Korea, Japan, Iraq, Peru, and Mexico, and has created language programs for companies such as General Electric (Brazil), LG (Korea), and Toyota (Japan).

He is the co-designer of the popular series *Teach English Now!* at http://www.coursera.org, where he helps thousands of aspiring teachers obtain a TESOL Certificate from Arizona State University.

He holds a doctorate in educational technology from Arizona State University and a master's in English (with an emphasis in language planning and policy) from Brigham Young University.

In addition, he is the author of the popular pedagogical text, *100 TESOL Activities: Practical ESL/EFL Activities for the Communicative Classroom.*

∾

Justin Shewell, Ph.D., Language and Education Specialist, Arizona State University

Dr. Shewell is the co-designer and primary producer for the largest TESOL certificate course in the world, *Teach*

English Now! This program, currently on the Coursera platform, boasts 250,000 learners from 194 different countries.

He has taught English in the Middle East, Asia, and the United States. He is the author of *50 Ways to Teach Online* along with several other book chapters and articles on language teaching and using technology in the language classroom. He is a regular presenter at international and regional conferences on language teaching and educational technology.

Dr. Shewell holds a Ph.D. in Educational Technology from Arizona State University and a Master's degree in Teaching English to Speakers of Other Languages from Brigham Young University.